The Christmas Script Book

Featuring
Star Light . . . Star Bright
and Other Plays for the Season

Compiled by Paul M. Miller

Contents

Star Light . . . Star Bright A drama for children by Paul M. Miller	2
The Shepherds' Christmas by Margaret Cheasebro	10
The Perfect Gift by Pam Hiscock (with Jim Nicoden)	23
I Heard a Call A monologue by Cindy M. Grant	41
What Happens at Christmas? A drama (with a choir) by Barbara T. Rowland	43

Lillenas Publishing Co.
Kansas City, MO 64141

Star Light . . . Star Bright
or
An Angel on Wheels

by Paul M. Miller

A Christmas play for children and teens that highlights courage as a gift of Christmas—even for a girl who is confined to her wheelchair.

Setting:

A church auditorium or sanctuary is the setting of this play. If a sanctuary is used, the chancel platform should be arranged so as to provide an acting area center stage.

Characters:

NARRATOR: a teen boy or girl
SUSAN: a teen Sunday School teacher
CAROL: a child in a wheelchair throughout the play
CHILDREN: as many as resources allow

    ROD   KANDY (ANGEL)
    TOMMY   BOBBY
    KARLA   TIM
    LISA   JENNY
    TERI

FIRST SHEPHERD
SECOND SHEPHERD   May be played by any of the above children
THIRD SHEPHERD
MARY
JOSEPH

(At rise: NARRATOR *enters. He stands center stage and speaks.)*

NARRATOR: The Word tells us that before Jesus was born in Bethlehem, people walked in darkness. The Bible says that there was bondage and unhappiness everywhere; that sin and sorrow took away joy and happiness. But then Jesus came; He brought sight to the blind, strength to the weak, healing to the crippled. Each of us here tonight should be reminded that Christmas is a happy recognition of what Jesus brings to us. Whether we are young or old or strong or weak or handicapped in some way, Christmas tells us that the Prince of Peace is here. He gives us joy. He gives us wholeness. And, as we learn this evening, He gives us courage.

(NARRATOR *exits.*)

Song – "We Wish You a Merry Christmas"

(CHILDREN *burst into the auditorium through all the doors in the room. They carry in cleaning supplies and decorating materials: ladder, dust mop, vacuum sweeper, garlands of evergreen, etc. While they work they laugh and sing a familiar, upbeat Christmas song [to be selected by the director]. At close of song...*)

ROD *(to everyone):* "Knock, knock."

TOMMY: "Who's there?"

ROD: "Snow."

EVERYBODY: "'Snow' who?"

ROD: "'Snow' what I want for Christmas?"

EVERYBODY: "What!"

ROD *(putting black wax over front teeth and singing):* "All I want for Christmas is my two front teeth..."

EVERYBODY *(ad-libbing):* Boo ... hiss ... etc.

(*Kids return to work and sing another verse of song. At end of verse...*)

KARLA: My turn. "Knock, knock."

EVERYBODY: "Who's there?"

KARLA: "Holly!"

EVERYBODY: "'Holly' who?"

KARLA *(singing operatically):* "O 'Holly' night, the stars were brightly shining..."

EVERYBODY *(ad-libbing):* Oh, no ... turn her off ... etc.

(*Kids continue working. They may sing another verse of song.*)

LISA: OK, listen to this one: "Knock, knock."

TERI: "Who's there?"

LISA: "Noah!"

EVERYBODY: "'Noah' who?"

LISA: "'Noah' what Tommy *really* needs for Christmas?"

EVERYBODY: What?

LISA *(singing):* "All he needs for Christmas is some mistletoe . . . some mistletoe . . . some mistletoe . . ." *(rest of* CHILDREN *interrupt with continuation of song).*

(Kids return to work and sing. SUSAN, *a college-age person, enters pushing a young girl down the aisle in a wheelchair. One by one the kids see her and stop singing. The song ends with a final lone group singing to the end without accompaniment. Then they, too, turn and see* SUSAN.)

SUSAN: Hi, kids. Sorry I'm late. Glad you went ahead without me.

EVERYBODY *(ad-libbing):* Hi, Carol . . . Hello . . . Merry Christmas . . . etc.

(CAROL *looks down at her hands with embarrassment.)*

SUSAN: I guess we ought to tell these people all about you, Carol. (CAROL *looks up at* SUSAN *and nods.)* You may or may not know that Carol is my cousin. She and her parents are missionaries in a country where things have gotten a little dangerous. Well, her folks thought it might be nice if Carol had Christmas here with my family and me.

BOBBY: That means Christmas with *all* of us!

TERI: And that calls for another "Knock, knock."

BOBBY: I've got one. *(To* CAROL) Carol, "Knock, knock."

(Everyone becomes very quiet. CAROL *looks embarrassed. She doesn't know how to respond.* SUSAN *saves the moment.)*

SUSAN: "Who's there?"

BOBBY: "Itsbee."

SUSAN: "'Itsbee' who?"

BOBBY *(singing):* "'Itsbee'-ginning to *sound* a lot like Christmas, since there's a Carol here . . ."

(CAROL *laughs and relaxes a bit.)*

SUSAN: Sorry, kids, but I've got to run home again. I forgot the costume box; and if we're going to be ready for our Shepherds' song, I'd better get it. *(To* CAROL) You look after the "flock," Carol. I'll be right back. Some of you run through the other song. And the rest of you, please help clean this mess up. I'll be right back.

(SUSAN *exits. The kids start to clean up. A group—or all—stand in choir formation and sing. One of the kids directs. At end of song, the group goes to* CAROL, *who has been listening to the rehearsal.)*

ROD: Well, hello, again.

CAROL: Hello. *(She looks shy.)*

KARLA: So, you came here for Christmas.

4

CAROL *(still looking down):* Yes.

LISA: What's Christmas like where you come from?

CAROL *(looking up):* It's a lot hotter than it is here.

LISA: Oh ... *(Awkward pause follows.* CAROL *looks down at her hands again.)*

TOMMY: Do you always have to sit in that ...

TERI *(interrupting):* Hush up, Tommy, you shouldn't ...

CAROL *(quickly responding):* Oh, that's OK. Everybody wonders about that.

TOMMY: Then, do you?

CAROL: Usually. This chair is kinda like my legs.

KARLA: How do you go Christmas shopping in it?

CAROL *(warming up):* Well, one time when Mama took me shopping in the capital, a man helped push me into an elevator—and the door closed before Mama could get in. So she took another elevator; but it went down and I went up. We never could arrive at the same floor at the same time. Finally Mama found me waiting in the Lost and Found. Now, every time we sing that song, you know, "I once was lost but now am found," my family has a big laugh.

(Everybody laughs.)

TIM: Are you going caroling with us after practice?

BOBBY: We're gonna have pizza and hot chocolate afterward.

CAROL *(unsure of herself):* Well ...

TERI: Sure she's going, and I'll push her.

TOMMY: No you won't. I will. That's a man's job!

LISA: Anybody see a "man" around here?

(Girls ad-lib looking for a "man." There is good-natured teasing; a general hubbub. Suddenly CAROL *calls out above the noise. She tries to stand and points toward a window.)*

CAROL: Look! Did you see it? Through the window—a falling star.

(All become quiet. Then CAROL *speaks...)*

CAROL *(with eyes closed):* "Star light ... Star bright ... First star I've seen tonight ..."

TERI *(with* CAROL*):* "I wish I may ... I wish I might ..."

EVERYBODY *(softly):* "Have this Christmas wish tonight."

*(*TOMMY *steps up to* CAROL*'s wheelchair.)*

5

TOMMY: What did you wish for, Carol?

TERI: Oh, Tommy, that's none of your business.

CAROL: I don't mind telling. I always wish for the same thing.

JENNY: Even when you blow out your birthday candles?

ROD: Or lose a tooth?

LISA: And when you see a falling star?

CAROL: That's right. But Christmas stars make it more special.

TOMMY: So, what did you wish for?

(*During this dialogue* SUSAN *enters carrying a box of costumes. She walks part way down the auditorium aisle, then stops and listens.*)

CAROL: I always wish that someday I'll be able to stand up and walk away from this chair.

(SUSAN *moves into the group. She stands by* CAROL *and strokes her hair.*)

SUSAN: What else do you wish for, Carol?

CAROL: At Christmas, I always wish that someday I could be the angel in the program—the one who says, "Don't be afraid! I have good news for you."

BOBBY: Well, why can't you?

CAROL: Whoever saw an angel roll in on wheels? Angels are perfect.

TERI: Charley was one of the three wise men last Christmas, and he had his broken arm in a cast.

CAROL: But that's not an angel!

KARLA: And remember when Jody's little brother was baby Jesus and he cried all through "Away in a Manger"?

ROD: Yeah, even through the part that says "No crying He made."

TOMMY: Know what I'd like to be in the Christmas program some year?

SUSAN: What's that, Tommy.

TOMMY: I'd like to be one of the animals in the stable where Jesus was born.

SUSAN: Which one?

TOMMY: I'd like to be the donkey that carried Mary from Nazareth to Bethlehem. I would be very careful and would get her there safely.

(SUSAN *takes* KANDY *by the hand and brings her over to* CAROL.)

SUSAN: Carol, this is Kandy. She is going to be the angel in our part of the Sunday School Christmas program.

CAROL: Oh, you'll make a wonderful angel.

KANDY: But, Carol, I'm so scared.

CAROL: But, Kandy, don't forget the words you get to say.

KANDY: You mean . . .

CAROL: "Don't be afraid! I have good news for you." Don't you be afraid, Kandy.

(SUSAN *gives* CAROL *a tinsel halo.*)

CAROL: Here's your halo, Kandy.

SUSAN: Now, Carol, let us show you our part of the Christmas program.

(CAROL *turns her wheelchair around and sits facing the stage from the floor level.* CHILDREN *take their places in choir area.* SUSAN *gives staffs and pieces of costume to three* SHEPHERDS—*may be boys and/or girls*—*who strike a pose as watching sheep. The* NARRATOR *stands to one side.*)

NARRATOR: On a very special night in Judea, a group of shepherds gathered on a hillside taking care of their sheep.

FIRST SHEPHERD: Oh, the night is *so* dark.

SECOND SHEPHERD: And our sheep don't want to go to sleep.

THIRD SHEPHERD: I wish something exciting would happen. I get so tired of these animals.

NARRATOR: All of a sudden there was a burst of light in the sky.

FIRST SHEPHERD: Look at that light!

SECOND SHEPHERD: What is it?

THIRD SHEPHERD: Why, it is an angel.

(SHEPHERDS *break out of character. They look at one another. It is obvious that the* ANGEL *is not going to make her appearance. The* CHILDREN *standing in the choir area crain their necks trying to see what is happening. There is whispering among the* CHILDREN. SUSAN *goes backstage and then reenters with* KANDY.)

KANDY: I'm sorry, Susan, but I'm just too scared.

SUSAN: Come over here, please, Carol. I want to share something with all of you.

(CAROL *wheels herself up to the stage. Other* CHILDREN *gather in around* CAROL *and* KANDY.)

SUSAN: Kandy and Carol have a lesson to teach all of us. Christmas is a time of joy, not fear. Carol has gone through some fearful days at home in her country. We are all concerned about her parents. Kandy is experiencing fear right now.

ROB: Well, I'm kinda nervous myself.

OTHERS *(ad-libbing)*: Me, too ... etc.

[*Staci*] SUSAN: Maybe we have been *wishing* on too many stars and not praying in the name of Jesus. Let's stop right here and pray that our fears will leave.

(Everyone bows his head. One by one CHILDREN pray. The director may use the script that follows, or allow the children to improvise their own prayers.)

[*Joel*] TOMMY: God, please help each one of us in our Christmas program.

[*Amber*] KANDY: Help me not to be afraid and to remember what I'm supposed to say.

[*Staci*] SUSAN: Be close to Carol's mother and father tonight. Keep them safe and give them Christmas joy.

[*Nick*] ROB: Please answer all of our prayers.

[*Holly*] CAROL: And, God, please answer my new friend Kandy's prayers.

EVERYBODY: Amen!

SUSAN: Places everyone. Let's pick it up from the angel's appearance.

(CHILDREN scurry into place.)

[*Kenny*] FIRST SHEPHERD: Look at that light!

[*Sean*] SECOND SHEPHERD: What is it?

(Angel enters the scene.)

[*Joey*] THIRD SHEPHERD: Why, it is an angel!

[*Amber*] ANGEL *(with great boldness)*: Don't be afraid, Shepherds, because I have wonderful news for you. A baby has been born in Bethlehem. He will be your Savior.

[*Eric*] NARRATOR: Then thousands and thousands more angels joined in praising God.

[*Kenny*] FIRST SHEPHERD: I'm not afraid anymore.

[*Sean*] SECOND SHEPHERD: Neither am I.

[*Song / Joey*] THIRD SHEPHERD: Then let's go see this child who has been born in Bethlehem!

"What Child Is This" 40

(All CHILDREN sing a Christmas song as SHEPHERDS move to a Nativity scene with MARY and JOSEPH at a manger. SHEPHERDS kneel. At close of song, SUSAN moves into the scene...) Nativity Scene Speaking Parts

Song - Silent Night
65
[*Staci*] SUSAN: Very nice, children. I think we are all ready for the program. Don't forget to ask your parents to invite their friends.

(CHILDREN busy themselves by putting things away and passing out the rest of the costumes. CAROL remains by herself on floor level with her back to the audi-

ence. SUSAN *goes over to her and turns her around to face the audience. She motions for the children to gather around* CAROL.)

KANDY: Thank you, Carol. You really taught me a lesson. I'm glad . . . We're *all* glad that you are here, Carol. You have been an angel to all of us. Here, please have my halo. *(She places halo on* CAROL's *head.)*

CAROL *(feeling halo):* Thank you, Kandy. I guess I'm an angel on wheels!

(KANDY *and the others exit down the auditorium aisle. From the back of the auditorium, the* CHILDREN *quietly sing a Christmas song.)*

CAROL: Star light . . . Star bright . . . Wondrous Christmas Child tonight . . . I promise You with all my might to trust You, who casts out fright. Amen.

(From the back of the auditorium comes TOMMY's *voice.)*

TOMMY: Come on, Carol. It's pizza time!

CAROL: Oh, this is going to be a wonderful Christmas after all.

(The CHILDREN *run back down the aisle.* TOMMY *pushes* CAROL's *wheelchair up the aisle. On their way out they call . . .)*

CHILDREN: "Merry Christmas to all . . . And to all a good night!"

NARRATOR: And a "good night" it was, for a girl in a wheelchair, her new friend who learned a lesson of courage, and a gang of boys and girls who better understand that Jesus came into this world for all people. That includes you who are in our audience tonight. The Child of Bethlehem will give you new life and the courage to face your world. Pastor _____, will you come and lead us in a prayer for Christmas life?

(PASTOR *prays, and the program may end with a congregational song.)*

(Blackout.)

The Shepherds' Christmas

by Margaret Cheasebro

Cast of Characters:
    JACOB: *a shepherd*
    NATHAN: *another shepherd*
    BARNABAS: *a third shepherd*
    BALTHAZAR: *a wise man*
    MELCHIOR: *another wise man*
    GASPAR: *a third wise man*
    HERALD ANGEL: *member of the heavenly host who speaks*
    MARY: *the mother of Jesus*
    JOSEPH: *her husband*
    EXTRAS: *any number of angels who are a chorus*

Props:
Colorful scarf, soft blanket, fur jacket or coat, manger, straw, baby doll, sandals, gifts for the wise men.

Setting:
The acting area on stage left will be the shepherds' field where the angel appears. The center stage area is the manger scene. The setting should appear as the entrance to a stable or cave. A blanket hangs over the doorway, which obliterates the audience's view of the interior, until the blanket is pulled back. This may be as elaborate or simple as the imagination or space limitations dictate.

(JACOB *and* NATHAN *enter from stage left.*)

JACOB: It's your turn to check the sheep, Nathan.

NATHAN: No, it's your turn. You made Barnabas do it when you should have done it last time.

JACOB: I traded with Barnabas. It's your turn.

NATHAN: You didn't trade with him. You just made him do it.

JACOB: That's what little brothers are for. Besides, he didn't mind. He likes to check the sheep.

NATHAN: You're just a lazy good-for-nothing shepherd boy. You don't care if the sheep get lost or not.

JACOB: I do, too. They're my father's sheep, and someday they'll be mine.

NATHAN: You don't fool me for a minute. You don't want to herd sheep when you grow up. You want to go to big cities like Damascus and Jerusalem and be a merchant.

JACOB: Merchants make lots more money than shepherds. And if I don't take over my father's flocks, Barnabas will. It does him good to learn everything he can about being a shepherd.

NATHAN: You'll never amount to anything, Jacob. All you do well is talk your way out of work. I'm glad you're just my cousin and not my brother.

JACOB: All you do is complain. Go check the sheep and leave me alone.

NATHAN: No, it's your turn.

(BARNABAS *enters from stage left.*)

JACOB *(points to* BARNABAS): There's Barnabas. He'll check the sheep for you.

NATHAN: Don't ask him.

JACOB: Barnabas, would you like to check the sheep for Nathan?

BARNABAS: I already did. They're fine.

NATHAN: Good boy, but you didn't have to. It's Jacob's turn.

BARNABAS: I know, but Jacob doesn't like to do it. So I did it for him.

JACOB: Thanks, little brother!

NATHAN: You're too nasty to have such a nice brother, Jacob.

JACOB: Everyone says Barnabas got his nice traits from me.

NATHAN *(cough, sputtering):* You're crazy.

BARNABAS: Quit arguing, you two.

(Sounds of bleating come from offstage. All three boys look toward left, where the sound came from.)

NATHAN: That sounds like a sheep in trouble.

BARNABAS: I hope it isn't Katrina. She just had a lamb. It's mine. Father said I could have the first one Katrina bore this season.

NATHAN: Quick, let's find out what's happening.

(NATHAN *and* BARNABAS *run off stage left.* JACOB *stretches out on the floor, his hands behind his head, his legs crossed lazily. His head is toward stage right, his feet toward stage left.)*

JACOB: Ah, this is the life. Nothing to do but enjoy the evening while those two dummies do all the work.

(From stage right the HERALD ANGEL *enters.* JACOB *is facing away from him and doesn't see him.)*

ANGEL: Jacob.

JACOB *(sits up, looks around but not behind him):* Huh? Who called my name?

ANGEL: Jacob.

JACOB *(sounding scared):* Who's there?

ANGEL: A messenger from God.

JACOB *(turns around, sees* HERALD ANGEL, *scrambles to his knees, looking scared):* I promise to take my turn at checking the sheep after this. Please, don't punish me.

ANGEL: I'm not here to punish you. Where are the other shepherds?

JACOB: They went to check on the sheep.

ANGEL: Go get them.

JACOB: Yes, sir.

(JACOB *hurries off stage left. While he is gone, the* HERALD ANGEL *motions for other angels to join him. They all enter on stage right and cluster behind him.)*

(NATHAN *enters on stage left, walking backward so he doesn't see the angels. He talks to* JACOB, *who is offstage.)*

NATHAN: If this is another one of your tricks, Jacob, I'll report you to your father when he comes to check the sheep in the morning.

JACOB *(enters stage left):* It's not a trick. Turn around and you'll see the angel. Oh, my goodness. Now there's more than one!

NATHAN *(turning around, looks startled):* Gracious! For once, you weren't exaggerating.

BARNABAS *(enters stage left):* Wow! Angels, just like you said, Jacob.

NATHAN: I've never seen an angel before.

BARNABAS: Me neither. Shall we kneel or something?

NATHAN: I don't know. Do you think they'll hurt us if we do the wrong thing?

ANGEL *(spreads out his arms):* Do not be afraid, for behold, I bring you good tidings of great joy which shall be to all people. For unto you is born this day in the city of David a Savior, who is Christ the Lord.

JACOB: A Savior?

NATHAN: How do we know this isn't a trick?

BARNABAS: Don't question him. Can't you see he's really an angel with a special message?

ANGEL: This will be a sign to you. You will find the Babe wrapped in swaddling clothes and lying in a manger.

ALL ANGELS: Glory to God in the highest, and on earth peace, good will among men.

(All ANGELS *exit stage right.)*

JACOB: Well, what are we waiting for? Let's check it out.

NATHAN: Bethlehem is only half a mile away. That must be where he meant, because it's the city of David.

BARNABAS: Yes, we must go. The angel wouldn't have told us if he didn't want us to see Christ the Savior, the Messiah.

NATHAN: But if we go, who will take care of the sheep?

JACOB: Not me. The angel appeared to me first. He must really want me to go.

NATHAN: I don't want to stay, and I'm sure Barnabas doesn't want to either.

JACOB: You'll stay, Barnabas, won't you?

BARNABAS: Well, I really want to come with you.

JACOB: We'll come back and tell you all about it.

NATHAN: Yeah, we'll fill you in on all the details.

BARNABAS: Oh, all right. Both of you go. I'll look after the sheep. I should probably keep an eye on Katrina and her new lamb, anyway.

JACOB: Good boy. You're the best brother a person could have.

NATHAN: Thanks, Barnabas. You're a real sport.

(JACOB *and* NATHAN *exit stage left.)*

BARNABAS *(sighs as he sits cross-legged in middle of stage):* Here I am again, alone with the sheep. I wish I weren't the youngest. Then I'd get to do more exciting things. But at least I got to see some angels. *(A sheep bleats offstage.)* I'd better check on that noise. *(He exits stage left.)*

(JACOB *and* NATHAN *enter from stage left and move slowly as though searching.)*

NATHAN: Here we are in Bethlehem, but I have no idea where to look.

JACOB: Look at that bright, bright star in the sky. *(Points to star over blanket by cave near stage right.)*

NATHAN: It's brighter than anything I ever saw.

JACOB: It seems to be pointing down to that cave over there behind the inn.

NATHAN: Let's check it out.

(They approach the cave entrance slowly, a little uncertain.)

NATHAN *(speaking)*: Knock, knock.

JOSEPH *(his voice can be heard from behind a blanket that covers the entrance to the cave)*: Come in.

(JOSEPH *pulls the blanket out of the way to reveal the cave's interior. In the cave is a manger in which the Baby Jesus sleeps.* MARY, JOSEPH, *and a donkey and some chickens are also there.*)

JACOB: An angel appeared to us tonight and told us we would find a baby wrapped in swaddling clothes lying in a manger and that He would be Christ the Lord.

NATHAN: We saw the bright star above your cave and thought maybe we'd find Him here.

MARY: You have come to the right place. Come, see the Baby. He's sleeping now.

(NATHAN *and* JACOB *move up to the manger and peer at the Baby. One stands on each side of manger, while* MARY *and* JOSEPH *stand together behind the manger.*)

NATHAN: He's so cute. He looks so tiny.

JACOB: Look at His tiny hands.

NATHAN: What do you call Him?

JOSEPH: His name is Jesus.

NATHAN: Hey, He's opening His eyes.

MARY: He seems to be looking for someone who isn't here.

JOSEPH: I wonder who He could be looking for?

MARY: I don't know.

NATHAN: Maybe He's looking for my cousin, Barnabas. He saw the angels, too, but he had to stay in the hills to watch the sheep.

MARY: Jesus is smiling. Barnabas must be the person He's looking for.

JOSEPH: Will one of you boys go get him?

JACOB: Not me.

NATHAN: If I go, I will have to stay with the sheep, and there will be no one to guide Barnabas here. Besides, I'd miss all this.

MARY: Jesus is looking at you, Jacob.

JACOB: Maybe that's because He wants me to stay.

MARY: I think He wants you to get Barnabas.

JOSEPH: I believe you're right, Mary.

NATHAN: Oh, come on, Jacob. I'll go with you. We can argue later about which one of us will guide Barnabas back here and which one will stay with the sheep.

JACOB: OK. *(Looks at* MARY *and* JOSEPH.*)*

NATHAN: Is He really the Messiah?

JOSEPH: That's what we've been told.

MARY: It's hard to believe, isn't it? He is so tiny in His bed of hay.

NATHAN: Come, Jacob. Let's get Barnabas.

(JACOB *and* NATHAN *exit stage left.* JOSEPH *drops blanket over cave entrance to conceal it. Then* JACOB *and* NATHAN *reenter stage left.)*

JACOB: I've told you over and over again, Nathan. I'm not going to stay with these sheep.

NATHAN: They're your father's sheep, Jacob. You're the one who should stay.

BARNABAS *(enters stage right):* I could tell you were back because I heard you arguing.

NATHAN: Hi, Barnabas. We found the Baby Jesus, and He wants to see you.

BARNABAS: Me? But how does He know about me?

JACOB: I don't know, but He's waiting for you, and I'm going to take you to Him.

NATHAN: No, you're not. You're staying with the sheep.

JACOB: We've already discussed this. I'm not staying with the sheep.

NATHAN: Yes, you are.

BARNABAS: Please, you two, stop arguing. Jacob, the sheep belong to our father. If he comes to make a surprise visit tonight and finds you're not with the sheep, you know how angry he'll be.

JACOB: He's only made one surprise visit in all the years I've been herding sheep. He only comes in the morning to check. He's as predictable as the rising sun.

NATHAN: This night is so unusual anything could happen.

BARNABAS: Please, Jacob. I don't want you to get in trouble with Father. You know how much it hurts him when you do something wrong.

JACOB: Oh, all right, I'll stay. But don't you two forget what a generous guy I am.

NATHAN: Let's go, Barnabas.

BARNABAS: OK. Everything's quiet, Jacob. All the sheep are doing fine. But could you check on Katrina and her lamb every now and then?

JACOB: Your lamb will be just fine. Quit worrying and get out of here, both of you, before I change my mind.

(NATHAN *and* BARNABAS *exit stage left.* JACOB *lies down with his hands behind his head, gazing at the night sky.*)

JACOB: Life is so unfair. Here I am lying around with these silly sheep and missing out on the biggest event that's ever happened here. I'll never let Nathan and Barnabas forget this.

(A noise, like someone walking, is heard offstage right.)

JACOB *(sitting up):* What's that? Oh, I hope it's not a thief coming to snatch the sheep. If anything happens to the sheep, Father will never forgive me. *(He stands up and looks apprehensive.)* Maybe I'd better go check.

(JACOB *walks toward stage right.* THREE WISE MEN *enter in a row.*)

GASPAR: Here's a lad who might be able to help us.

MELCHIOR: Ah, good, a lad.

BALTHAZAR: But he's just a shepherd boy.

JACOB *(proudly):* I am Jacob, heir to my father's flocks. Please be quiet so you won't disturb the sheep.

GASPAR: Sorry.

MELCHIOR: Yes, sorry.

BALTHAZAR: Cocky little shepherd, isn't he?

GASPAR: We have come from the East on a long journey, following the star that will show us where the Messiah has been born.

MELCHIOR: The Messiah.

BALTHAZAR: Why bother asking this shepherd? He probably doesn't even know what the word "Messiah" means.

JACOB: Of course I do. He is the promised deliverer of the Jews. And I know where He is.

GASPAR: You do?

MELCHIOR: You do?

BALTHAZAR: I'll be a camel's caretaker. You surprise me, boy.

GASPAR: Don't mind Balthazar. We've been traveling a long time, and he gets grumpy when he's tired.

MELCHIOR: Yes, grumpy.

BALTHAZAR: Who's grumpy? Not me. But I'll tell you this, Gaspar. If I were leading this group, we'd already be there.

GASPAR: Can you tell us where to find the Babe?

JACOB: Yes. *(Pauses)* For a fee.

GASPAR: What is your fee?

MELCHIOR: Yes, what?

BALTHAZAR: The little scheming thief!

JACOB: Three silver coins.

MELCHIOR: Three silver coins?

GASPAR: Three silver coins.

BALTHAZAR: Three silver coins!? That's robbery!

GASPAR: How about one silk scarf?

JACOB: It will take more than that.

MELCHIOR: And one soft blanket.

JACOB: What else?

BALTHAZAR: And one kick in the pants.

(JACOB *folds his arms in front of him in a gesture of disgust.*)

GASPAR: Come now, Balthazar. Surely you can spare something.

BALTHAZAR: Oh, all right. How about one jacket made from the skins of foxes.

JACOB *(unfolds his arms):* Show me these things, and I will decide.

(*All* THREE WISE MEN *bring him what they mentioned and with a flourish spread them in front of* JACOB, *who carefully looks them over.*)

JACOB: Your gifts are acceptable. I will tell you where the Messiah is.

GASPAR: Wonderful.

MELCHIOR: Yes, wonderful.

BALTHAZAR: Start talking.

JACOB: He sleeps in a manger in a cave behind the inn at Bethlehem.

GASPAR: In a manger?

MELCHIOR: In a cave?

BALTHAZAR: Behind the inn? What a liar you are, boy. No Messiah would be born in such a terrible place.

JACOB: It's true.

BALTHAZAR: Give back that jacket, you little criminal.

GASPAR: Patience, Balthazar. He may be telling the truth.

JACOB: I saw Him tonight. My cousin and I went to see Him after the angel told us where to find Him.

BALTHAZAR: An angel? His story gets more and more ridiculous. Let's take the boy and sell him as a slave in Damascus.

GASPAR: We have come a long way to find the Messiah, Balthazar. Let's not mar the trip with talk of taking slaves.

MELCHIOR: No slaves.

BALTHAZAR: Be thankful, boy, that's all I have to say.

GASPAR: Point the way, shepherd.

JACOB *(points to stage left):* Bethlehem is that way. Everyone knows where the inn is. The cave is behind it. You will find the Babe there as I told you.

BALTHAZAR: If we don't find Him, we'll be back to get you.

MELCHIOR: Yes, back to get you.

GASPAR: Don't threaten him. You drive a hard bargain, boy. You could have a future as a merchant.

(The THREE WISE MEN *exit stage left.)*

JACOB: He said I had a future as a merchant. (JACOB *picks up the scarf, blanket, and jacket and hugs them to his chest.)* And here's my start. Whoopee! I'd better hide these before Nathan and Barnabas get back so no one will know I have them. They are my ticket out of this little town to the big city and a merchant's life.

(JACOB *jubilantly exits stage right.* NATHAN *and* BARNABAS *enter stage left.)*

NATHAN: I don't see Jacob. I'll bet that lazy brother of yours left the sheep all along.

BARNABAS: Maybe one of them had trouble, and he went to check on it.

NATHAN: Not Jacob. He doesn't care one bit about those sheep.

BARNABAS: We'd better check the animals. I hope nothing happened to Katrina or her lamb.

(As NATHAN *and* BARNABAS *walk toward stage right,* JACOB *enters stage right.* JACOB *looks momentarily startled, then quickly recovers.)*

JACOB: Oh, hi, Barnabas and Nathan. I didn't think you'd be back so soon.

NATHAN: We were gone long enough to have a good visit with the Baby and His mom and dad.

BARNABAS: The Baby sure is cute. He smiled at me.

NATHAN: He smiled at you almost all the time. I think He liked you a lot.

JACOB: How come? What's so special about Barnabas?

NATHAN: Maybe Jesus likes the way Barnabas takes such good care of the sheep and is willing to do more than his share.

BARNABAS: I don't mind taking care of the sheep. I like them. Jesus was probably just smiling to be smiling.

JACOB: If you were having so much fun with the Baby, how come you came back so soon.

NATHAN: Barnabas wanted to give the Baby something.

JACOB: But, Barnabas, you don't own anything except the clothes you're wearing. What are you going to do, give Him your old stinky sandals?

BARNABAS *(looks down at his sandals):* No, they're not good gifts for the Messiah. I need something very special.

JACOB: Dream on, little brother.

NATHAN: Your brother is right this time, Barnabas. You don't have anything to give the Baby.

BARNABAS: Yes, I do.

JACOB: What?

NATHAN: Yeah, what?

BARNABAS: I can give him Katrina's lamb.

NATHAN: Your lamb?

JACOB: But you love that lamb. You talk about it all the time.

BARNABAS: It's all I have, and I want to give the Baby something very special.

JACOB: But the lamb needs its mother's milk now. If you took it away from Katrina, it would die.

BARNABAS *(sadly):* Then I have nothing to give the Baby Jesus.

NATHAN: Don't look so sad. I'm sure Jesus understands what you want to do and why you can't.

BARNABAS: Why couldn't I be older? Then the lamb would be older too, and I could give it to Jesus. (BARNABAS *dejectedly moves toward stage left and sits down with his head in his hands.)*

NATHAN: I've never seen your brother look so sad, Jacob.

JACOB: Me neither. I know I'm sometimes mean to Barnabas and make him do more than his share of work. But I really love him.

NATHAN: I know you do. So do I. I just wish I had something to give him so he'd have a gift for the Baby Jesus.

(NATHAN *looks at* JACOB.)

JACOB: Don't look at me. I don't have anything to give Him either.

NATHAN: I know. We're all the children of poor shepherds, and we'll probably always be poor. Still, I wish I had something to give the Baby.

(JACOB *paces back and forth as though wrestling with a problem.*)

NATHAN: What's wrong?

JACOB: It's . . . nothing. *(Sighs deeply.)*

NATHAN: Something's wrong.

JACOB: No.

NATHAN: You can't fool me. I know you too well.

JACOB: Oh, I might as well tell you. I'll never feel right about it if I don't.

NATHAN: Did something happen to the sheep?

JACOB: No, they're fine.

NATHAN: Did you leave them unattended?

JACOB: No, it's nothing like that. It's just that . . . well . . .

NATHAN: I'm listening.

JACOB: See, these three wise men came by while you two were gone.

NATHAN: Wise men?

JACOB: Yeah, they were all dressed up in fancy clothes, and they came from somewhere faraway.

NATHAN *(puts his hand on* JACOB's *forehead):* Are you sure you're not running a fever or something?

JACOB *(backs away):* Cut it out, Nathan. You've got to believe me. They were looking for the Baby Jesus.

NATHAN: Did you tell them where to find Him?

JACOB: Yes, but . . . well . . . I, that is, I . . . well, I made them pay for the information.

NATHAN: You did?

JACOB: Yeah.

NATHAN: You have a lot of nerve.

JACOB: It was real easy. One of them told me I drove a hard bargain and had a future as a merchant.

NATHAN: Are you sure you're not making this up?

JACOB: It's true.

NATHAN: It sounds like something you'd dream up. I mean, really, am I supposed to believe that both angels *and* wise men visited you tonight?

JACOB: I know it sounds fantastic, but it's true. Wait here, and I'll prove it to you.

(JACOB *exits stage right while* NATHAN *makes motions that show he thinks* JACOB *is crazy.* JACOB *immediately returns with the jacket, blanket, and scarf.*)

JACOB: See? They gave me these.

NATHAN *(shocked expression on his face):* Goodness gracious. You were telling the truth. These are beautiful.

JACOB: I know. I thought I could hide them and use them to help me become a merchant. But I can't do it now, not when I see how sad my brother is.

NATHAN: So what are you going to do?

JACOB: I'm going to let him choose one of these to give the Baby.

NATHAN: I owe you a big apology, Jacob.

JACOB: You do?

NATHAN: I underestimated you. The Jacob I thought you were never would be this generous.

JACOB: It does seem crazy, doesn't it? *(Calls to his brother.)* Barnabas, come here.

BARNABAS *(looks up from his sitting position. Speaks sadly):* I'm coming. *(He walks over to* JACOB *and* NATHAN. *Perks up when he sees what* JACOB *has.)* Where did you get these things?

NATHAN: The wise men gave them to him.

BARNABAS: Did you steal them?

JACOB: No. Wise men really did give them to me. They came by tonight and asked where the Baby was. I made them pay for the information.

BARNABAS: That sounds like you. These are beautiful. *(He touches the scarf.)* I love the colors in this scarf.

JACOB: Then it's yours.

BARNABAS: Mine?

JACOB: Yes, yours.

BARNABAS: You're giving this to me? *(Reaches up to feel JACOB's forehead.)* Are you sure you're feeling all right?

JACOB *(backs away):* Cut it out, Barnabas. The scarf is yours.

BARNABAS: Thank you, thank you, thank you. Now I have a gift for the Baby Jesus!

JACOB: Nathan, now you choose one.

NATHAN: Me?

JACOB: Yes, you.

NATHAN: Well, I really like the blanket.

JACOB: Then it's yours.

NATHAN: I don't know how to thank you. Now I have a gift for the Baby too.

JACOB: And I'll give Him the jacket.

BARNABAS: Look, the sky is getting light. It's almost morning.

NATHAN: That means our fathers will be coming soon to check on the sheep.

JACOB: Maybe they will watch the sheep while we go visit the Baby.

BARNABAS: I'm sure they will.

NATHAN: I see them coming now. I'll run and ask them if we can go.

(NATHAN *exits stage right. While he's gone,* BARNABAS *and* JACOB *admire the gifts.* NATHAN *reenters stage right.)*

NATHAN: They said yes. Let's go.

JACOB: Good deal!

BARNABAS: Aren't you sad to give up your treasures, Jacob?

JACOB: I thought I would be, but they've made you so happy that it makes me happy too. And if I could drive a hard bargain with the wise men, I can do it again with someone else.

NATHAN: I know you'll be a good merchant someday, Jacob.

BARNABAS: Let's go! I can hardly wait to see the Baby Jesus' face when we give Him these presents.

(All exit stage left. Center stage is illuminated. JOSEPH *pulls back the blanket over the cave/stable door. Each of the characters enter the scene and stand at the manger:* MARY, JOSEPH, *and the* HERALD ANGEL. *Other* ANGELS *enter and take place at manger.* THREE WISE MEN *enter and bring their gifts to Jesus, then stand stage left. The* THREE SHEPHERDS *enter, put gifts by manger, then stand beside the* WISE MEN. *All bow, then say in chorus, "Hallelujah, Jesus is born!")*

The Perfect Gift

by Pam Hiscock (with Jim Nicoden)

Characters:

SALLY
CLERK
BOSS
MANNEQUIN NO. 1
MANNEQUIN NO. 2
MANNEQUIN NO. 3
MANNEQUIN NO. 4
LADY
STORE SPEAKER (VOICE)
MAN NO. 1
MAN NO. 2
EXTRAS
PATTY
CHRIS
MOM
DAD

Act 1

SALLY *(in front of the curtain):* Christmas is a time for giving. That's what my teacher told me in school. And this Christmas, I'm ready to give. I've been saving my allowance for weeks, and I bet this year, I can buy the best gifts my family's ever seen. I have *(She takes a handful of change out and counts.)* $5.25. I bet I can buy a whole bunch of gifts with that much. I especially want to buy my dad a nice gift this year. Daddy says I'm his little girl. I'm special to him... and he makes me feel special. So this year, I want to make him feel special. I want Daddy to be so happy on Christmas morning when he opens my present. So I'm off to the department store to find him the perfect gift.

(Curtain opens. Stage is set for a department store... Bustling people... Christmas music coming over speakers. When SALLY *talks to the* CLERK, *everyone freezes.* SALLY *walks into the store wide-eyed.)*

SALLY: Wow!! I'm sure I can find the perfect gift for Dad here!

CLERK: Hello there! May I help you with something?

SALLY: Yes, please. I'm looking for a present for my dad.

CLERK: Well, we certainly have some nice things here.

SALLY: But nice isn't good enough. He's a very special dad, and I need something *great*.

CLERK: How about giving him LOTS of things, then, to show him how much you love him?

SALLY *(wide-eyed):* Lots of things??

CLERK: You could give him a present on each of the 12 days of Christmas.

SALLY: Twelve days?? When did Christmas become 12 days? I think Santa Claus has been cheating me. He only came on one day to my house.

CLERK: Let me show you some of our merchandise . . .
> **On the first day of Christmas**
> **your first present could be . . .**
> **A silk tie for $12.93**

SALLY: $12.93?? But I have only $5.25. And that would only buy one present, and I'd still have 11 days of Christmas to go . . . and I don't even like your ties.

BOSS *(yuppie-looking, comes out and watches what is going on. Clears throat):* Excuse me, Mrs. Gerberstein. May I have a word with you??

CLERK: Just a minute, Mr. Stanford. I'm with a customer.
> **On the second day of Christmas**
> **your present could be . . .**
> **Isotoner gloves . . .**

BOSS: **She's not spending any money!** *(Drags CLERK off to the side.)*

CLERK: Mr. Stanford, you always tell me that the customer comes first.

BOSS: That's when there's no one else who needs your help in the store. Let me put it this way. There are only a few more shopping days until Christmas. This store is mobbed with people who have lots of money to spend. Don't take up all your time with a little girl. Spend time with other customers. I'll take care of the little girl.

CLERK: Yes sir. *(She walks off.)*

BOSS: Little girl, why don't you just shop on your own. I'm sure you're big enough that you can find what you're looking for all by yourself. *(Walks off.)*

SALLY: But . . . but . . . I want to get something that's perfect. *(She frowns.)* How can I do that without any help?

MANNEQUIN NO. 1: Psst . . . hey . . . psst. Little girl.

(SALLY looks around, looks at the MANNEQUIN NO. 1, then looks around again.)

MANNEQUIN NO. 1: Little girl! Hey! It's me.

SALLY *(looks at the MANNEQUIN NO. 1 coming to life):* It *is* you! But how can you talk? You're just a store dummy!

MANNEQUIN NO. 1: Hey kid! Watch your language. What did I ever do to you, huh?

SALLY: Sorry!!

MANNEQUIN NO. 1: Do you want help with a present, or what??

SALLY: Yeah, I sure do!! That lady only got to the second day of Christmas, and I missed hearing what the other 10 days were, and I didn't even like the first 2!

MANNEQUIN NO. 1: Hey, kid, take it easy. I can let you in on the other days.

SALLY: You can?? Oh, good. I was getting worried that I was never going to find the perfect gift for my dad.

MANNEQUIN NO. 1: The thing you've gotta keep in mind when shopping for your dad's present is . . . fashion.

SALLY: Fashion??

MANNEQUIN NO. 1: Sure!! You said your dad is extraspecial, right? (SALLY *nods.*) Then he must be very fashion conscious!

SALLY: I don't know. Do you have to be "fashion conscious" to be a great dad?

MANNEQUIN NO. 1: Of course you do, kid! What's the matter with you, don't you watch television? Haven't you seen the commercials?

SALLY: Well, sure, but . . .

MANNEQUIN NO. 1: Then you know that every truly "together" man is making some sort of fashion statement!

SALLY: If you say so. But what does this have to do with my getting my dad the perfect present?

MANNEQUIN NO. 1: It's just that a man of truly classy taste will appreciate a truly fashionable gift. Now you said that you didn't like the first two presents that stodgy ol' Mrs. Gerberstein showed you, right?

SALLY: Yuk!!

MANNEQUIN NO. 1: Sweetie, don't say "yuk" just yet! I admit that she showed you the very worst and oldest in colors and prints, but the merchandise isn't that bad!!

SALLY: It's not??

MANNEQUIN NO. 1: No! Think of a silk tie . . . but in an up-to-date paisley print, instead of a plain navy blue!! Or the gloves in a chic dark black color instead of stodgy brown!

SALLY: Well, I don't know. Can you tell me about the other presents for the other days of Christmas?? Maybe I'll like one of them.

MANNEQUIN NO. 1: OK, kid, I know you're going to love them. Ya ready??

SALLY: Sure!!

MANNEQUIN NO. 1 *(he looks around):* I just need to be careful. They don't know I can talk yet. They think I'm just a poor working stiff *(chuckle)* . . . Get it? OK, coast is clear . . .
> **On the third day of Christmas**
>   **your present could be**
> **Rolex for men,**
> **Isotoner gloves,**
> **and a silk tie for $12.93.**

SALLY *(talking while music continues):* Rolex for men? Are they expensive? Are they extraspecial??

MANNEQUIN NO. 2 *(coming to life):* Hey!! I want some of the attention!
> **On the fourth day of Christmas**
>   **your present could be**
> **Cotton oxford shirts,**
> **Rolex for men,**
> **Isotoner gloves**
> **and a silk tie for $12.93.**

SALLY: Hey! TWO of you can talk??

MANNEQUIN NO. 1: **On the fifth day of Christmas**
>   **your present could be**
>   *(Here the other 2* MANNEQUINS *come to life and join in in harmony.)*
> **14-karat rings**
> **Cotton oxford shirts**
> **Rolex for men**
> **Isotoner gloves**
> **and a silk tie for $12.93.**

SALLY: WOW! Have you guys ever thought of making a record??

MANNEQUIN NO. 4: Do you think it's really good???

SALLY: You sound just like real people singing!

MANNEQUIN NO. 2: Hey, guys, we might be able to work our way out of this dumpy department store someday, after all!

SALLY: You guys are so good you could even sing in commercials!

MANNEQUIN NO. 3: Would you like to hear our version of "Moon River"? Or how about "Basin Street Blues"? *(They begin to get pitches and start singing.)*

MANNEQUIN NO. 1: Wait a minute! If we're going to go into singing commercials as "The Mannequins," we've forgotten to ask the most important question. Did we sell the customer? OK, little girl, did you like our fashionable new products??

SALLY: Well . . . not really. Oh . . . it's not you . . . you sounded terrific. But my dad . . . he's extraspecial. And somehow I want to give him something more meaningful than a tie or gloves!!

LADY: Excuse me, little girl? *(All* MANNEQUINS *freeze.)*

SALLY: Yes?

LADY: Who were you talking to?

SALLY *(turns around to point to* MANNEQUINS, *and sees that they are frozen again):* Nobody in particular. It's just that I'm upset because I can't find the best gift to give my dad!

THE STORE SPEAKER: Attention, shoppers! Wondering what to buy that special person on your Christmas list?? For the next five minutes we're going to be having a sale in the gourmet shop. All coffeepots 40% off. But only while they last!!

LADY: That's it! That's what you can get your dad and I can get my husband!! *(She grabs* SALLY's *arm and starts to drag her to the "Gourmet Shop.")* But we have to hurry!

SALLY: Why would I buy a coffeepot?

LADY: BECAUSE IT'S ON SALE!!!!

SALLY: But I don't think my dad needs a coffeepot.

LADY *(she stops, obviously frustrated):* Little girl, where did you get the money to buy your dad's Christmas present?

SALLY: From my allowance.

LADY: And who gives you your allowance?

SALLY: My mom and my dad.

LADY: Then I'm sure that they'll appreciate your buying something that's on sale! (SALLY *still looks puzzled.)* Oh, I give up. If you want to come with me to get the coffeepot, then fine. But if not, I only have 2½ minutes left to get there. Bye!!

SALLY *(sighs, then looks up to see a* MAN *standing next to her looking at electronics):* Hey, mister? If you had a little girl about my age, what would you want her to buy you for Christmas?

MAN NO. 1: Well, I don't have a girl your age . . . so I'm not quite sure. Really the only thing that I want this year is this pocket calculator that keeps track of my budget. Look at it . . . isn't it great? If I buy $10.00 worth of food, then

I plug in $10.00, then the code for food, and it immediately registers under food. Now, I haven't quite figured out how to add up all of the amounts in the food column yet. Actually, I'm not even sure how to recall the $10.00 yet. I wonder if when you turn it off, if all of the information disappears? That wouldn't be very helpful. I wonder if there's a better model around? Or maybe I should just buy the software for my computer to do this. Still, then I wouldn't be able to carry it around in my pocket and immediately add each item in as I bought it . . . *(He continues talking to himself.* SALLY *shakes her head and walks away.)*

SALLY *(sees* MAN NO. 2 *in the sporting goods department):* Hey, mister? What about you? What do you really want more than anything else this Christmas?

MAN NO. 2: That's easy. I want to get in shape.

SALLY: But you have a nice circle-shape already.

MAN NO. 2: That's my problem. I'd like to have a nice rectangular shape. Or maybe even triangular. Big muscular shoulders coming down to a tightly defined waist.

SALLY *(trying to make herself into the shape of a triangle):* How do you figure you can make yourself into a triangle?

MAN NO. 2: Well, for starters, I'm buying these fancy running shoes. I'm going to start myself on a jogging program. I bet in no time at all I'll be running 10 to 20 miles a day.

SALLY: Wow!! How far do you jog now?

MAN NO. 2: Jog? Well . . . uh . . . I don't . . . that is, I don't YET . . . but as soon as the holidays are over, you watch, I'll be out there running.

SALLY: Sure . . . *(She walks away.)* People sure are weird . . . *(Everyone is frozen.)* But at least I've gotten some more ideas for what to give my dad. Let's see, by now, I must have *(counts)* eight ideas. *(This time the song is sung in a sparse, hollow way. There are breaks between lines, and each person sings his own line alone. Everyone is frozen until they sing, then they freeze again, except for the little girl who turns and listens to each of the gifts.)*

>**On the eighth day of Christmas**
>**my present could be . . .**

MAN NO. 2:	**Running shoes for jogging . . .**
MAN NO. 1:	**Calculator adding . . .**
LADY:	**Coffeepot a-perking . . .**
MANNEQUIN NO. 1:	**14-karat rings . . .**
MANNEQUIN NO. 2:	**Cotton oxford shirts . . .**
MANNEQUIN NO. 3:	**Rolex for men . . .**

MANNEQUIN NO. 4: **Isotoner gloves . . .**

SALLY: **Or a silk tie for $12.93.**

(She sighs.) No . . . none of those gifts is right. I need something more exciting.

MAN NO. 1 *(coming over to her):* Little girl, you asked me what *I* wanted for Christmas. The reason my answer was a calculator is because this particular kind of calculator is one of the few electronic gadgets that I don't already have. But if you're looking for a gift for your father . . . how about the latest in VCRs?

MAN NO. 2: Or, if you really want excitement . . . how about an exercise bicycle?

MANNEQUIN NO. 1: No, no, no . . . if you want a truly phenomenal present, get him something from Pierre Cardin . . . even a simple belt—100% top grain designer leather, mind you—is an exquisite gift from Pierre Cardin. *(Everyone in the store is looking at the MANNEQUIN come-to-life.)*

MAN NO. 2: I didn't know you could talk.

MANNEQUIN NO. 1: Not only do I talk, but I sing.

MANNEQUIN NO. 2 *(coming alive):* Would you like to hear US?? *(Uproar as people in the store are discussing the MANNEQUINS.)*

SALLY: Wait, wait! What about me? I still need to find a present.

MAN NO. 1: What's wrong with our suggestions?

SALLY: Well, first of all, I don't think any of them are special enough . . . none of them is the perfect gift. But also, can I buy all this stuff for $5.25??

BOSS: Little girl, if you only have $5.25 to spend in cash, I know what you can get for your dad.

SALLY: What?

BOSS: A credit card to charge all of these things!! *(Everyone nods in agreement.)*

SALLY: This is dumb.

CLERK: This is great! Now you have all 12 days of Christmas . . . Everybody!!

(Everyone begins to sing, the verses get faster each time [until No. 5]. There is lots of movement, wildness in general!)

EVERYONE SINGS: **On the twelfth day of Christmas,
your present could be
Credit card for charging . . .**

SPORTS DEPARTMENT: **Exercycle biking . . .**

MANNEQUINS: **Leather belt for buckling . . .**

ELECTRONICS DEPT.:	**VCR recording . . .**
SPORTS DEPARTMENT:	**Running shoes for jogging . . .**
ELECTRONICS:	**Calculator adding . . .**
BARGAIN HUNTERS:	**Coffeepots a-perking . . .**
MANNEQUINS:	**14-karat rings . . .**

(The MANNEQUINS *break into a shoo-bop rendition of 14-karat rings . . . instrumentals and more shoo-bop type of music goes for a while.* SALLY *begins to back offstage, with a puzzled/frightened look on her face.* MANNEQUIN NO. 1 *spots her going off.)*

MANNEQUIN NO. 1: Hey! Little girl!! Where are you going? *(Everyone on stage stops and looks at* SALLY.*)*

SALLY: Umm . . . well . . . I'm going to find the perfect gift for my dad. I haven't found it here.

MANNEQUIN NO. 1: What's wrong? Don't you like my paisley ties???

LADY: What about the coffeepots??

MAN NO. 1: Or the VCR?

MAN NO. 2: Or how about the exercycle??

(All four groups— MANNEQUINS, BARGAIN HUNTERS, ELECTRONICS DEPARTMENT, *and* SPORTS DEPARTMENT*—begin to chant their particular product ["paisley ties" . . . "coffeepots" . . . "VCR" . . . "Exercycle" . . . "paisley ties" . . . "coffeepots" . . . etc.] and begin to converge on* SALLY *as they chant. When they are almost surrounding her,* SALLY *screams and runs offstage. Comments from people being like "Some people just can't handle shopping" OR "I wonder where her Christmas spirit is??" OR "I just don't understand why she didn't get the bargain coffeepot . . . I think that's a special gift." They all go back to "shopping," [which means they go offstage] . . . curtains close, but the* MANNEQUINS *are in front of the curtain.)*

MANNEQUIN NO. 2: I wonder why she ran off like that . . . I thought she liked our singing!

MANNEQUIN NO. 3: She said she did. Hey, do you guys think that we could really make it in commercials?

MANNEQUIN NO. 1: WE won't unless we practice! Let's take it from five again. Ready? *(They sing the last five days as they walk offstage.)*

END OF ACT 1

Act 2

(The setting is a living room ... may be in front of the stage curtain.)

SALLY *(running in, out of breath)*: You'll NEVER believe what happened to me at the store!!

PATTY *(sitting on a sofa with feet up, reading "Seventeen," not paying any attention to her sister)*: Uh-huh.

SALLY: I went to find the perfect present for Dad, and the store dummies came to life and talked and sang and then ...

CHRIS *(also looking through a magazine ... possibly sports)*: Yeah. And then I bet that everyone in the store started dancing.

SALLY: How did you know?

CHRIS: You REALLY expect me to believe you??

SALLY: Don't you believe me? I'm telling the truth!

CHRIS: Listen, Sis. If you're going to tell stories, you should at least learn to tell ones that are half believable!

SALLY: Honest! I'm telling the truth! And then I ran and ran because I didn't want the stuff they showed me and it was too expensive and I didn't like it anyway.

PATTY *(closing the magazine angrily)*: Honestly! What a pain-in-the-neck-of-a-kid-sister you are. I'm trying to read my magazine, but you come in babbling about who knows what ...

SALLY: My present ... my perfect gift for Dad.

CHRIS: What perfect gift?

SALLY *(exasperated)*: That's just it! I haven't got one!

PATTY: You haven't got one. And you're looking for one? But why are you worried? All of your gifts in the past have been soooo good. What about the soap on the rope?

CHRIS: Yeah! That was a great gift. It made Dad smell like a pine tree for months afterward. Pew!

PATTY: Then there was that charming paperweight that you made him.

CHRIS: It looked like an ugly lump of clay to me.

PATTY: Or how about the ...

SALLY: I know, I know, I know! All my gifts in the past haven't been good enough. But come on—please help me think of the perfect gift for this year! I need some ideas. What does Dad REALLY want?

PATTY: How should I know what Dad really wants?

(SALLY *sits down with a sigh, and looks like she might begin to cry.*)

PATTY: OK, OK. I'll try and help you think of something. What about a book?

SALLY: Too boring.

PATTY: How about cologne?

SALLY: Too smelly.

PATTY: A pair of socks?

SALLY: Still too smelly.

PATTY: How about some tools?

CHRIS: Hey, yeah!! I've been trying to get him to fix my bicycle for weeks but he says he doesn't have the right tools. You could get him the tools, and then he could fix my bicycle!

SALLY: No, that's not the kind of present I want!

PATTY: Hey, if I showed you what I bought for him, do you think that would help?

SALLY: Hey, yeah! It might help.

PATTY *(goes over behind couch and picks up a box):* This is a great present . . . it's right in style. I might borrow it from Dad if there's ever a day when he doesn't wear it. It's . . . *(opens box and holds up)* a silk paisley tie!

SALLY: By any chance, did it cost you $12.93?

PATTY: Did I leave the price tag on it???

SALLY: No . . . it's just that I . . .

CHRIS: Hey! Don't you want to see what I bought Dad??

SALLY: Sure . . . it can't hurt.

CHRIS *(taking it from behind the couch):* It's . . . a coffeepot!

SALLY: WHY are you giving Dad a coffeepot?

CHRIS: Because it was on SALE!! You don't think I'm going to spend my whole allowance on a present, do you?

SALLY: You just don't understand.

CHRIS: Besides, I don't see what the big deal is about buying Dad a Christmas present anyway. Don't you know that what you get is more important than what you give? I can't wait until I get my new softball glove. I'll have all winter to soften it up, and then when we start practice in the spring, I'll be the best second baseman Kennedy Junior High has ever had!

PATTY: How do you know you're getting the glove you asked for?

CHRIS: I found it in Mom's closet before she wrapped it.

PATTY: Hey, is there any stuff there for me?

CHRIS: Naw. Your stuff is hidden under Mom's bed.

(PATTY *starts to run out of the room to find her Christmas presents.*)

SALLY: Wait! What about me? I still need help finding the perfect present for Dad!

PATTY *(turns):* What about all our suggestions?

SALLY: They're just not special enough. *(She shrugs and looks at the floor.)*

CHRIS: Thanks a lot.

SALLY: They're just not perfect.

PATTY: That makes us feel really good. Our presents aren't good enough.

CHRIS: Brat!

SALLY: I'm sorry. It's just that . . .

PATTY: You want some PERFECT ideas?

SALLY: Oh, please. I KNOW you can help me. I know you'd have some good ideas if you really wanted to.

PATTY: OK, I'll help you. I have some ideas about what Dad would really like . . .

        **You want a present
        That's the perfect one?
        Here's some suggestions . . .
        Pick one when I'm done.**

        **Why don't you promise
        To keep quiet all year;
        Stop all your babbling,
        Give rest to our ears.**

CHRIS: **Give rest to our ears
                We'll thank you for years
                Keep quiet all year and
                Give rest to our ears.**

SALLY: **Keep quiet all year?
                How can that be done?
                You're not being fair
                'Cause I'm the youngest one!**

PATTY: The perfect present
          That's the one you want
       I've heard our dad say
          Peace and quiet he wants.

       Or how about this?
          This one's better by far,
       Be perfect all year,
          Be Dad's little star!

SALLY: Be perfect all year?
          How can that be done?
       You're not being fair
          'Cause I'm the youngest one.

CHRIS: Be perfect all year
          We've nothing to fear
       The perfect gift's near
          Being perfect all year.

PATTY: Why don't you promise
          To do everyone's chores
       From laundry to windows.

CHRIS: You could even do floors!

PATTY: You could scrub and clean
          You could iron and press,
       Then we wouldn't complain
          When you made the mess.

CHRIS: Scrub and clean
          Iron and press
       Wouldn't complain
          If you made the mess.

SALLY: Do everyone's chores?
          How can that be done?
       You're not being fair
          'Cause I'm the youngest one.

PATTY: Now there's a good point,
          You're the youngest one.
       That makes me remember
          Dad wanted a SON!

SALLY: Dad wanted a son?

CHRIS: Dad wanted a son.
       We can remember
       Dad wanted a son.

SALLY: That really can't be
>That's not really true
You're just being mean
>I don't believe you!

PATTY: I know that's what Dad
>Really wants more than all
I heard him tell Mom
>That day in the mall.

SALLY: What day in the mall?

CHRIS: That day in the mall
That day in the mall
That day in the mall.

PATTY: A few days before
>You arrived on the scene
I heard Dad say this,
>(Now don't think I'm mean).

He whispered to Mom
>As we bought baby toys
I really want this one
>To be a boy.

SALLY: To be a boy?

CHRIS: To be a boy.
He wanted this one
To be a boy.

PATTY: Now don't get me wrong,
>Now of you he's fond,
But what he'd really love
>Is a boy that's blonde!

SALLY: Blonde?

PATTY: Blonde.

CHRIS: Blonde.
Blonde.
What he'd really love
Is a boy that's blonde.

SALLY: I can't be a blonde
>I can't be a son
How will I find a gift
>That's the perfect one?

> How can I be perfect?
> How can I be neat?
> For a whole year long
> How can I stay sweet?
>
> I'd love to give Dad
> All these things and more
> To do all for him
> To buy him the store.
>
> To work, work, and work
> So I'd prove to him
> How special he is
> How much I love him.
>
> To find the perfect gift...
> How can that be done?
> It's just not fair,
> I'm the youngest one!

END OF ACT 2

Act 3

(SALLY *is in her bedroom, rocking a dolly and singing the last verse of "Away in a Manger" [which has been the instrumental transition between the two acts]. She sighs.*)

SALLY: So, dolly, you don't have any ideas for a Christmas present for Daddy either, huh? *(She listens.)* I didn't think so. *(She starts to cry.)*

MOM *(coming into room)*: Good night honey. Sally? Honey, what's wrong?

SALLY *(sobbing)*: I can't find the perfect present!

MOM: What perfect present?

SALLY: For Daddy! I wanted to get him the perfect present and so I went to the department store but couldn't find it there. And then I asked Patty and Chris for ideas, and they said that Dad wanted a...son...or that I should try and be perfect all year, and do everyone's chores...and I know I can't do that, and...

MOM: Oh, honey...shh...don't listen to them. And don't worry. You've always gotten wonderful presents for Dad before. Like last year...the uh...what was it?

SALLY: Soap-on-a-rope.

MOM: Soap-on-a-rope. That's it. That was a wonderful present. It made Dad smell so...so outdoorsy.

SALLY: But it wasn't perfect.

MOM: I know that you want to get Dad the perfect present, and that's good, but what's more important is that . . . well, listen. I have a story to tell you that I think will explain what I mean, OK?

SALLY *(nods and lies down):* OK . . .

MOM: **The Little Drummer Boy**
Honey, do you understand what I'm trying to tell you?

SALLY *(sleepily):* Uh-huh . . .

(MOM *tucks in* SALLY, *kisses her, and then creeps offstage.)*

SALLY *(sits straight up in bed):* But I don't even play the drum! Now what am I going to give Dad? *(She begins to cry again. The lights dim and the toys in her room come to life. [Toys: Raggedy Ann, Ballerina, Teddy Bear, Toy Soldier, and Baby Doll]* BABY DOLL *goes over and taps* SALLY *on the shoulder.)*

SALLY *(looks up):* Baby Doll! I'm so sad. I can't find the perfect present for my dad.

(BABY DOLL *motions to the toys.)*

SALLY: You . . . do you have some idea??

(BABY DOLL *nods, then walks over with the other toys. They each dance alone and with* SALLY.)

(BALLERINA *ends by bowing to* SALLY.)

(BABY DOLL *and* RAGGEDY ANN *dance together, they swing* SALLY, *they go around in a circle, etc., and then end by flopping on the floor with their arms open wide [in doll-like fashion] to* SALLY.)

(TOY SOLDIER *ends up giving* SALLY *his drum.)*

(TEDDY BEAR *ends up giving* SALLY *a bear hug.)*

SALLY: Oh, teddy . . . and all of you. Thank you so much. Thank you for your dance . . . and your hugs . . . and your drum . . . and your love. I feel so much better. Except . . . except that I still don't have a present for Dad. Hey, wait a minute! You've all given me an idea. You each made me feel better because you gave me your love. What I need to give Daddy is me. I need to let him know that I'm his no matter what happens . . . that I love him with all my heart. That's a better gift than anything! And I know how I'll tell him, too!

(SALLY *goes over to her desk and takes out paper and crayons, etc., as the toys crowd around. Lights dim; transitional music.)*

END OF ACT 3

Act 4

("Joy to the World" is sung as transition into ACT 4. As the lights come up [and the song is still being sung], the family is opening presents. DAD *opens the tie and the coffeepot,* CHRIS *hits her glove, etc. This is all pantomimed. As the song ends . . .)*

DAD: This was a wonderful Christmas morning! Thank you all for all of your wonderful presents!

CHRIS: Dad, you never opened Sally's gift.

DAD: Well, I didn't, did I? I must have missed it. *(He begins to look around.)*

SALLY *(embarrassed):* I still have it.

PATTY: Well, come on! Let's see it! I can't wait to find out what the "perfect gift" is.

SALLY: I don't know.

DAD: What's wrong, honey?

SALLY: Oh, Daddy, it's not a real fancy present, or expensive, or . . . oh, I don't know. I really mean what it says. But it's kind of . . . dumb.

DAD: Can I see it?

(SALLY *brings out a box, which* DAD *unwraps.)*

DAD *(opening the box, he takes out a picture of a heart, and inside is a letter, which he reads):*
Dear Dad:
    This Christmas I wanted to find you the perfect present, because you're the perfect dad. So I looked everywhere. And I thought about all the things that I could do for you. But nothing was perfect enough. So this Christmas I don't have a tie to give you or even soap-on-a-rope, because they weren't right.
    But what I do have this Christmas to give you is me. That might sound dumb, because I already am your girl, but what I mean is, I want you to know that no matter how old I get, or how far away I live, and no matter how I change or you change, I love you, and I trust you, and I owe you everything. I'm completely yours, Dad.
    Love,
        Sally
(DAD *is choked up.)* Sally, that's beautiful. This is the nicest Christmas present I've ever gotten, or could ever get.

SALLY: Really??

DAD: Honey, I love you. *(He gives her a hug.)* Thank you so much.

CHRIS: Next year, I'm drawing a heart on a piece of paper. It's a lot cheaper than a coffeepot!

PATTY: If he doesn't want my tie, I wish he'd tell me. I love it!

DAD: Hey, kids! Sally's gift reminds me of what Christmas is all about . . . God's perfect gift to us.

SALLY: What was that, Dad?

DAD: God give himself to us.

SALLY: You mean Baby Jesus?

DAD: It sure was. And do you know what God wants from us more than anything else?

PATTY: I don't know what one thing He wants, but I give him lots. I'm kind to everyone, and I go to church. I even helped collect food for people at Thanksgiving, and I'm a GREAT sister.

DAD: Patty, those things are good, but they're not what God really wants most of all.

PATTY: Dad, what more could He ask for?

DAD: Sally, what do you think?

SALLY *(who has been thinking hard this whole time)*: ME???

DAD: That's it. He just wants you.

SALLY: Wow!

CHRIS: Can we go eat Christmas dinner now? PLEASE? I'm starving!

DAD *(laughs)*: If it's ready.

MOM: It's ready! Come on!

(Everyone exits except SALLY, *who sits there thinking, and* DAD, *who is about to leave until he sees* SALLY *not moving.)*

DAD: Honey? Are you coming to dinner?

SALLY: Dad? You said what God really wants is me, right?

DAD: That's right.

SALLY: Well, then, since it's not only Christmas, but it's Jesus' birthday, do you think that maybe I should give Him a present?

DAD: I think that's a great idea.

SALLY: Dad, would you be upset if, besides giving me to you, I gave myself to Jesus, too?

DAD: I wouldn't mind at all.

SALLY: Merry Christmas, Jesus!

Jesus, Merry Christmas

THE END

I Heard a Call

by Cindy M. Grant

It all began one day with a strange visit. Talk about earth-shattering news! There I was—16 and pregnant. Then when I told my parents . . . it was not a happy day in Nazareth! At first they didn't believe me. An angel's visit? A virgin birth? But they knew I loved God. They knew I would answer His call.

Then came the ridiculing: the whispers behind veils . . . the snickers at the well. Of course, no one believed the story. And I must admit, it was a bit unbelievable. But even close friends rejected me. Old ladies shook their heads as they passed me, even protecting the young from my shadow. But I paid no attention for I . . . I heard a call.

No one really understood . . . except for Joseph. Ah, wonderful Joseph. It wasn't easy for him, either. Everybody thought he should have put me away privately. I'm thankful that God sent His angel to Joseph, too. He obeyed. It wasn't easy for us, but I knew the child I carried was the Son of God. Imagine! ME—being chosen to bear God's Son. I had no idea then what would lie ahead, but I knew it wouldn't be easy for my son, either. So I obeyed because . . . I heard a call.

After Jesus was born, the angel warned us about King Herod. I couldn't understand why he wanted to kill this innocent child. I didn't know he was only the first of many who would feel threatened by Jesus. God told Joseph to take us to Egypt, where we would be safe. I was so frightened during that trip. What if we were caught? We would all be killed. But, then, I remembered the angel's words. "He shall be great, and shall be called the Son of the Highest: and the Lord God shall give unto him the throne of his father David: And he shall reign over the house of Jacob forever; and of his kingdom there shall be no end." I didn't know what all that meant at the time, but I knew God's will could not be accomplished if Jesus were killed as a baby. I knew God would spare Him. But my heart still ached for all the mothers whose sons were ripped from them by a maniac who thought he could kill the plan of God. When it was safe, we returned to Nazareth. I had no idea we were fulfilling prophecy. We just answered the call.

Those childhood years were so special. Such a unique child. So loving and caring and tender. He always wanted to help. He always seemed to *know*. I loved watching him work with Joseph in his shop. His little hands would hold the tools so carefully as he handed them to Joseph. Then that trip to Jerusalem. I'll never forget how upset I was when I discovered that Jesus was not among our friends in the caravan. I worried about him all the way back to Jerusalem. I was so angry! How could he just run off like that and let me worry? Sure, he said we should have known where to find him, but I was furious. He was usually so considerate, so thoughtful. How could he do this? And he, a child of 12, just looked me in the eye and repeated, "I was doing my Father's business." It was then that I knew. I knew that the rest of his life, he would be doing his Father's business. I also knew that he would never be understood—anymore than I understood him that day. The road would never become easy. But I still heard a call.

When he got ready to leave home, he tried to explain to me. I'm not sure I understood his purpose any more then than I had 30 years earlier when the angel tried to tell me. But I trusted him. I knew he had to answer his call.

Oh, the emotions that filled me during those years. The pride. The love. The fear. I think I remember every miraculous story that ever found its way to my ears! He did so much good. And to think that the hands that once wrapped around my finger now touched the blind and the lame, and they were healed!

And then the end. All the lies, the accusations, the betrayals from friends. And then the worst day on earth ... the day I watched them kill my son. Sure, he was the Son of God. But he was MY SON! I bore him. I nursed him. I kissed him when the human body he had chosen to take on was hurt. When they drove those nails into his hands, I could hardly bear the pain. Then I heard a call. "Woman, behold thy son!" Even in his dying moments, when his body was wracked with pain, he was taking care of the needs of others. He was taking care of me.

His death was so horrible. And his resurrection so miraculous! The news spread like wildfire. Some, of course, doubted. "Alive? It can't be!" But I knew better. For *I* knew Jesus.

Well, that was many, many years ago. I've lived to see my son's teachings spread, in spite of opposition, in spite of persecution, against all odds. And I have faith that his message will live on until he comes again. Many years ago I answered his call. And today ... today I hear another call. "Mother, come on home." I am coming, Son! I am coming!

What Happens at Christmas?

A Drama with a Choir

by Barbara T. Rowland

Cast:

DAUGHTER: *a teenage girl with lots of energy who wants to be a foreign exchange student and who likes shopping*

SON: *a college-age boy who is bored with home life and above it all*

MOTHER: *a gushing, sweet, tradition-bound woman who directs the family*

DAD: *a good ol' boy who wants to do right by his family and who speaks with a strong regional accent*

GRANDMOTHER: *a feisty woman who loves her family and who speaks her mind*

STUDENT: *a teenage girl who is an exchange student from a country—likely behind the Iron Curtain—which does not observe Christmas and who wants to know what happens at Christmas*

MINSTREL: *opens the play—may be played by the choir director*

SALESPERSON

SALVATION ARMY PERSON

Scene List:
Scene 1: Airport waiting room, a week before Christmas
Scene 2: Shopping mall the next day
Scene 3A: Kitchen, a few days later
Scene 3B: Son's bedroom, same day
Scene 4: In car on the way to Christmas Eve service
Scene 5: In living room on Christmas morning
Scene 6: Same as Scene 5

Prop List:
Backpack, shoulder bag, and coat for STUDENT in first scene.
Optional: Other characters may wear jackets depending on December weather in area of performance.
Ticket for STUDENT to hand DAD.

Handbags for two girls in Scene 2. Jewelry and cards are pantomimed. Bell to ring and container for coins for SALVATION ARMY PERSON.

Two stools, aprons for MOTHER and GRANDMOTHER, bowl with pecans and nutcracker for GRANDMOTHER, bowl and spoon for MOTHER in Scene 3. Stool and telephone for SON in Scene 3B.

Scene 4 actors may add jackets for dress. DAD needs a coat. Six chairs or stools are needed.

Two stools, some empty boxes and wrapping paper, Bible, decorated Christmas tree, and robes for the four women are needed for Scenes 5 and 6.

Setting:
There are no set pieces. Play is performed on platform in sanctuary with choir in place the entire time. Cast may sit on first pew and enter from there. Props are placed by actors.

Scene 1

(MINSTREL *enters and goes to microphone in center of stage. Costume is not necessary. Guitar is optional.*)

MINSTREL: What's the reason we rejoice?
　　　　　What's the cause we celebrate?
　　　　　Why the lifting of our voice?
　　　　　Why the reverence of this date?

　　　　　Is it for the gifts we get?
　　　　　Is it for the family near?
　　　　　Is it for the customs set
　　　　　That we keep from year to year?

　　　　　As we ponder on these questions
　　　　　And on the birth of a baby boy,
　　　　　Let children begin our celebration
　　　　　Singing songs of Christmas joy!

(Children's Choir sings.)

MINSTREL: Tonight we've come together
　　　　　For a Christmas celebration.
　　　　　Let's observe and then see whether
　　　　　Our Lord is honored by tradition.

　　　　　Suppose a person came to see
　　　　　What happens here at Christmastime.
　　　　　Would his observation prove to me
　　　　　That we rejoice in the birth sublime?

(MINSTREL *exits. If played by choir director, he goes to position in choir loft. If played by a layman, he sits on front pew during play.*)

(*Family rushes on from stage right. May come from first pew.* DAUGHTER *leads, goes down center and looks front eagerly.* MOTHER *and* GRANDMOTHER *follow hurrying and stop up left of* DAUGHTER. FATHER *and* SON *saunter up right. All look front.*)

DAUGHTER: The plane is landing! I told you we should've left for the airport sooner. We could easily have been late.

MOTHER (*soothingly*): Now, now, relax. We're not late. She won't know we barely made it.

GRANDMOTHER: Not unless we tell her. (*Shocked looks from* MOTHER *and* DAUGHTER.) Which, of course, we won't. I'm glad I got here for Christmas before this exchange student. Did you barely meet my plane?

FATHER: What does it matter? We made it, didn't we? Timing's just right for this one, too. Opening the doors on the plane now. No use sitting 'round the airport. Planes generally run late anyways.

SON (*complaining*): Why couldn't this foreigner wait until after the holidays to come and move in? I just get home from college and somebody—

DAUGHTER (*interrupts*): Don't call her foreigner! Now you be nice. She doesn't even celebrate Christmas in her country and we want this one with us to be special. Oh, look—people are getting off—

FATHER (*talks to* SON *as the three women watch anxiously for expected guest to get off plane*): Well, Son, this was just how the school terms worked out is why she's a-comin' at Christmas. You know your sister wants to BE a foreigner—that's why we're havin' one. (*Laughs at his joke as* SON *looks bored.*)

MOTHER (*she and* GRANDMOTHER *ease up on line with* DAUGHTER *as they watch.* MOTHER *points straight ahead*): I'll bet that's our girl!

GRANDMOTHER: Sure enough! She's carrying a lot and looks—well, different!

DAUGHTER: It is! I know it is. Move back everybody. She'll come in over here and I get to speak first.

(MOTHER *and* GRANDMOTHER *move up and right as* DAUGHTER *crosses left of center to meet exchange* STUDENT *who comes on platform from front pew slightly left of center. She wears heavy coat and has a shoulder bag and backpack.* DAUGHTER *moves to her.*)

DAUGHTER: Hi! I'm your American sister.

STUDENT (*English is slow and careful, not a distinct country accent although suggests behind Iron Curtain*): Hello. Thank you for meeting me.

DAUGHTER: And this is my family. (*Turns and gestures to others.*) Your family, too, for a while. (*Family acknowledges introduction almost at once.*)

MOTHER: Glad you're here safely.

GRANDMOTHER: So nice you came in time for Christmas.

BROTHER *(slightly inclined head):* Hi.

FATHER: Mighty proud to have you, gal! Now, you jes' give me your suitcase tickets and Son and I will go get 'em.

(STUDENT *looks at* DAD *questioningly. Everyone glances from one to another.* MOTHER *speaks in a loud voice as if to a deaf person while* DAD *makes pantomime motions as if holding two suitcases.* DAUGHTER *touches backpack.)*

MOTHER: Your baggage, dear.

STUDENT *(with sudden recognition):* Oh, yes. *(Takes ticket with attached baggage claims from pocket and hands to* DAUGHTER *who passes them to* DAD.*)* Thank you.

FATHER *(takes ticket and with jerk of head indicates* SON *is to go with him):* We'll see y'all out front.

DAUGHTER *(reaches for* STUDENT*'s shoulder bag):* Here. Let me carry some of that.

MOTHER *(speaks loudly again):* Was your trip tiring? Oh, I know it was. Such a long way. Did you have a long wait in Dallas? *(Insert name of nearest international airport.)*

STUDENT *(looks steadily at her as she speaks. Seems unclear until she says "Dallas"):* Dallas! Oh, yes. Pretty. Lots of people and lots of—like a party—what do you call—oh, yes—decoration. Pretty. *(Pause.)* Why?

GRANDMOTHER: It's Christmastime! You've come to America at Christmas. It's the very best time of the year.

MOTHER: Come on, girls. Let's go. Probably the bags are here by now and your Father will be waiting. (MOTHER *and* GRANDMOTHER *exit stage right. Go to first row of pews.)*

DAUGHTER *(as she and* STUDENT *start to follow and then stop):* Yeah. What you saw were Christmas decorations. Lots of lights and stuff? Christmastime is fun!

STUDENT: Christmas? Christmas we don't do in my country. What happens at Christmas?

DAUGHTER: What happens? Well, lots of things. *(Brightens)* My favorite part is shopping. We do lots of shopping at Christmas. See, we buy things for everybody. You can go to the mall with me tomorrow and see what happens at Christmas! *(Girls exit same way others did.)*

(Blackout.)

Scene 2

(Lights come up on youth choir behind acting area in regular choir loft. Sing light Christmas music. When music is finished, lights off choir and on acting area. If not using lights, choir simply sits. Girls enter center right from front pew. Two people may come from the choir to be extras in scene. One goes stage left and one stage right. Turn backs until needed.)

STUDENT *(looking around):* This is the shopping place? It's so big! What do you call it?

DAUGHTER: Mall. It's a shopping mall. See, lots of stores are together under one roof. Aren't the Christmas decorations beautiful? *(Gives a little shiver.)* I love to come here this time of year. Shopping is my favorite part of Christmas.

STUDENT: So this is what happens. *(Brightly as if understanding.)* Everyone comes here and has a party!

DAUGHTER *(laughs):* No, not exactly. We come and buy gifts for our family and friends. And they buy gifts for us! I love getting presents, don't you?—Hey, come on. *(Takes her arm and pulls her stage right to person there.)* I need to look at this jewelry.

SALESPERSON *(turns around. Stands slouchy and chews gum):* Watcha need? Kin ah hep ya? *(Runs together.)*

STUDENT: What did she say?

DAUGHTER: That's just a phrase they teach salespeople. Means nothing. *(To* SALESPERSON*)* Naw, jes lookin'. *(To* STUDENT*)* That's what you say back to them. (SALESPERSON *turns away. She picks up earrings.)* These earrings aren't bad—and they're cheap, too.

STUDENT: You get the Christmas shopping gifts as cheap as you can?

DAUGHTER: Well, I buy some extra gifts in case someone gives me one I hadn't thought about. I have extra gifts for an emergency.

STUDENT: Is confusing. Is like a game and you guess who buys for you? Why is it emergency?

DAUGHTER *(irritated with explaining and with how it sounds):* Never mind the details. Just enjoy the shopping. *(To* SALESPERSON*)* I want three of these.

SALESPERSON: That'll be $6.98.

(DAUGHTER *pantomimes giving her a bill and receiving change. Puts change and earrings in purse quickly. Moves down center stage with* STUDENT *on next line.)*

DAUGHTER: Let's go over there to the card shop now. I haven't found a special enough one for Joe yet.

STUDENT: This is a big job, this shopping.

DAUGHTER *(girls are down center and* DAUGHTER *begins to look at cards):* I guess. But you gotta give to get, seems like. So you could look at it like you're shopping for yourself and that makes it even more fun. Look at the cards. (DAUGHTER *picks up card, reads it, shakes head and puts it back.)*

STUDENT *(has looked over fronts of cards without picking up any):* There is a word I do not know on many cards. What is r-e-j-o-i-c-e?

DAUGHTER *(uninterested):* Oh, you see that a lot at Christmas. It's "rejoice."

STUDENT: What does it mean?

DAUGHTER *(preoccupied with looking at cards):* It means to be glad.

STUDENT: To be glad? Use it for me so I can remember.

DAUGHTER: Oh, like—REJOICE in the gifts you get at Christmas. Let's go. I can't find one for Joe.

(Girls walk stage left. SALVATION ARMY PERSON *rings bell.* STUDENT *is startled.* DAUGHTER *is bored.)*

STUDENT: What is she selling?

DAUGHTER: Nothing. Just asking for money for the poor. I've got some change from getting jewelry. *(Drops coins and goes past person.)*

SALVATION ARMY PERSON: God bless you. Rejoice in Jesus!

STUDENT *(watches in fascination. Eagerly catches up with* DAUGHTER *and stops her):* Did you hear? She used the word I just learned!

DAUGHTER *(shrugs. Suddenly brightens and waves off stage left):* There's Betty and Jill. Hi! Wait for us. Isn't shopping fun?

(DAUGHTER *rushes off stage left pulling* STUDENT *with her.* STUDENT *glances back at* SALVATION ARMY PERSON.)

(Blackout.)

Scene 3A

(Choir sings song reflecting scene. May change word STUDENT *learns if select song with another appropriate word. Lights come up on choir for song, dim out at finish. Before lights come up on acting area,* MOTHER, GRANDMOTHER, STUDENT, *and* SON *take places. The three women are center stage.* MOTHER *wears apron and pantomimes stirring.* GRANDMOTHER *sits on high stool stage right of her, holds a bowl and pantomimes shelling nuts.* STUDENT *sits on stool stage left of* MOTHER. SON *is far stage left with telephone ready for next scene. Lights up center stage.)*

MOTHER: This is what happens in the kitchen at Christmas. Cooking! There is so much to do. I have the fruitcake, some pies, and decorated cookies in the freezer. I did all that early. But now I have to make the cinnamon rolls and arrange them like a Christmas tree for us to eat Christmas morning. Son would be so disappointed if I didn't. Why, we've had our homemade sweet-roll tree every Christmas morning since he can remember.

GRANDMOTHER *(eagerly):* And I made it for you when you were a girl. Remember how you liked to decorate the tree? Sprinkled it with little sparklies. Did Son ever like to do that?

MOTHER: No. He just likes to eat it!

STUDENT: So this is what happens at Christmas for American women? This cooking is what it is all about?

MOTHER *(defensive):* Well, that's not all, of course. But that's what is expected of us. Why we'd feel guilty if we didn't make all these things.

STUDENT *(stands, crosses to* GRANDMOTHER *who hands her a bite of pecan):* But—is more than we can eat!

GRANDMOTHER: Of course. Always. We wouldn't feel we had done our job unless we had lots of choices and more than enough.

STUDENT: Christmas is a big job.

MOTHER: It IS an awful lot of work. American mothers are supposed to produce Christmas for their families, though. We wouldn't feel right if we didn't.

STUDENT *(crosses back to stool on first part of line):* It is a PRODUCTION? I am glad I came before it so I could watch. I want to understand what happens at Christmas.

(The three women freeze. Lights out on them. Spot up on SON *stage left. He sits on stool and talks on phone.)*

Scene 3B

SON: Yeah. I know what ya mean. Nuthin' to do in this town. I'll be glad to get back to college where we can party.—Only good thing about the holidays is sleeping late and not going to class.—Sure, we have a blast all the time.—Naw! You didn't! Hey, that's cool.—Oh, same ol' thing over here. Mom is creating her cute cinnamom roll Christmas tree. We always have it. *(Sarcastic)* Borrring. Hey—one new thing. We've got a foreigner here. Girl exchange student from somewhere. Never celebrated Christmas before. Weird.—Yeah, I know—nothing good on TV with all the dumb Christmas specials. Tell me about it!—Nothing happens around here at Christmas. Boresville.

(Blackout.)

Scene 4

(Lights up on choir. Selection should reflect meaning of Christmas.)

(When lights come up on acting area, all six characters are in a car going to a candlelight Lord's Supper on Christmas Eve. FATHER *drives,* MOTHER *and* GRANDMOTHER *are in front with him.* SON *is behind* FATHER, DAUGHTER *is in middle, and* STUDENT *is next. Actors may use stools with the three back ones slightly taller. Pantomime driving and riding.)*

STUDENT: This going to church—this is something that happens on eve of Christmas all over America?

DAD: Land sakes, no, child. Just a few of us who really know what Christmas is all about go to worship services. Why, millions of Americans aren't Christians and millions of the ones who are don't let it interfere with their Christmas parties. Why, we're among a minority who truly keep the religious holiday.

SON: Don't know why we ALWAYS have to go, Dad. None of my friends do. Looks like we could forget church during the holidays.

DAUGHTER: Yeah. I wanted to open presents tonight, but, no. We have to go to church and have a family dinner. *(Pouts.)*

GRANDMOTHER: Now, children, don't forget WHY we celebrate this day in the first place.

MOTHER: She's right. Remember the real reason for Christmas. Oh. Did we tell you the reason for all that happens? *(She is asking* STUDENT *in seat behind* GRANDMOTHER.*)*

STUDENT: No. But I know lots of things you DO about it!

DAD: But all the other things are just extra. It's a religious holiday and we remember the story in the Bible—let's see, where is it? *(Asks* MOTHER.*)*

MOTHER: It's in Luke, dear.

SON *(sarcastically):* Yeah. We read it every year.

DAUGHTER: I learned most of it by heart once in Sunday School!

DAD: Wish that car would go on or get out of the way! I don't want to be late for the service. *(Honks horn.)* Oh, as I was saying, see we remember the story about a baby born a long time ago who grew up to be the Son of God. And that's why we celebrate. Now, maybe I can get around him here. *(Pantomimes passing car.)*

STUDENT *(interested):* The Son of God? But that's—remarkable. Do you believe it? That story, I mean.

MOTHER: Of course, we do.

STUDENT: I want to read that story. Do you have this book it is in?

SON: Just about 10 of them. What version you want?

GRANDMOTHER: Don't be tacky. We have a chance to tell her the gospel of Jesus Christ.

DAUGHTER: Well, I guess that would be a good thing to tell her at Christmas.

DAD: Would ya lookit that! That guy got our parking place. We always park there.

MOTHER: Perhaps it's a visitor. Go on around to the lot.

STUDENT: Did the people know when He was born that He was the Son of God?

GRANDMOTHER: Some of them did. Mary, his mother, knew and some shepherds on a hillside knew.

DAD: Here's one—if I can cut in before that other car—now! OK, gang. Y'all hurry so we can get our pew 'fore someone else does.

(All reach for door handles and freeze as STUDENT speaks wonderingly toward audience.)

STUDENT: How could they KNOW who he was?

(Blackout.)

Scene 5

(Actors carry stools and exit to front pew. Lights up on choir. Sing appropriate song. When music is finished, lights out on choir and have few counts of darkness as cast sets scene. Place Christmas tree up center. Lights on if possible. MOTHER *sits left of tree.* GRANDMOTHER *sits slightly down right.* FATHER *stands right of tree.* STUDENT *and* DAUGHTER *sit on floor down center amid empty boxes and wrapping paper.* SON *stands stage left. There is an air of depression.)*

SON: Well, I guess that's that. Whose turn to carry out the trash?

DAUGHTER: I just knew Joe would give me something—slip it under the tree when I wasn't looking. But no! He's a bum!

MOTHER *(to* GRANDMOTHER*)*: Guess they enjoyed the Christmas tree cinnamon rolls all right. At least they ate them. *(Sighs.)* Lots of effort for an INHALED breakfast.

GRANDMOTHER: Well, you feel better for having made it, dear. Thanks for my lovely robe. *(Holds up top of robe from box in her lap.)* I know I'll enjoy it.

DAD: I want us to have a family time today. We have Son home and Grandmother with us and we're sure proud to have an extra daughter.

SON *(upset):* Whatda ya mean, Dad? I got plans.

DAD: Not today. You can spend one day out of your school holidays with your family. And this is it!

(SON *groans.*)

STUDENT: I would like to read that story you started to tell me last night. The one about the baby born and it was the Son of God.

MOTHER: Oh, that's a great idea. Let's read her the Christmas story from the Bible! That would be a lovely family thing to do this morning.

DAD: Sure would! Hand me that Bible from the bookshelf, Daughter, and I'll read it.

(DAUGHTER *rises, gets Bible from choir rail back of* MOTHER, *and gives line and finds scripture as she crosses to* DAD.)

DAUGHTER: You'll find it in Luke 2. Here it is.

(Family settles to hear story. SON *and* DAUGHTER *look bored.* GRANDMOTHER *and* STUDENT *are interested.* MOTHER *has a sweet smile.* DAD *gets into it as he reads from King James Version, Luke 2:1-11.)*

DAD: ". . . For unto you is born this day in the city of David a Saviour, which is Christ the Lord."

(Blackout.)

Scene 6

(Family freezes while choir sings. DAD *sits on stool, which he puts in place at first of scene so that his head isn't in the way. Tree lights stay on while choir sings. When music is finished, lights out on choir and back up on family scene.* DAD *stands and closes Bible.)*

DAD: That's what Christmas is all about. We celebrate the birth of Jesus Christ.

GRANDMOTHER: But not just the birth. To read only that part is like starting a book in the middle and then wondering why you don't understand the story.

MOTHER *(to* STUDENT*)*: That's right! To know why Christ's birth was so important you need to know about God's promises all through the Old Testament to send a Savior to be a sacrifice for the sins of us all.

STUDENT *(has been listening intently):* Jesus was expected to come?

DAUGHTER: Yeah. But you see, nobody thought He'd come like He did. People thought He'd come like a king.

SON *(has started listening):* Remember that time He came into Jerusalem like a king just before He got crucified? I was a disciple walking in with Him in an Easter play once.

DAD: Ya, see, Hon, the rest of the story is that He made some folks mad 'cause He said He was the Son of God and they put Him to death when He was 33 years old. But He rose from the dead and is alive still!

GRANDMOTHER: God's plan is that we accept Jesus' payment on the Cross for our sins and have a relationship with God. We were created for that. So, the important thing that happens at Christmas is the life that Jesus came to give us. We can claim it—or renew it—at Christmas.

STUDENT: THAT is what happens at Christmas? But—that's so wonderful!! Does everybody know it? *(Full front as others all look at her.)* Does everybody KNOW what can happen at Christmas?

(Blackout.)

(Lights up on choir. If possible, leave some light on scene as actors hold places for final number.)

(MINSTREL steps to microphone. Spot on him. Dim or out on choir and scene.)

MINSTREL: What's the reason we rejoice?
        What's the cause we celebrate?
        Why the lifting of our voice?
        Why the reverence of this date?

        Is it for the gifts we get?
        Is it for the family near?
        Is it for the customs set
        That we keep from year to year?

        What happens in this holy season?
        Is Christ the Savior in us reborn?
        May God's love be the reason
        We rejoice this Christmas morn!